# THE KNOWN WORLD

WESLEYAN POETRY

# THE
# KNOWN
# WORLD

## Don Bogen

WESLEYAN UNIVERSITY PRESS
Published by University Press of New England • Hanover and London

WESLEYAN UNIVERSITY PRESS
Published by University Press of New England, Hanover, NH 03755
© 1997 by Don Bogen
Printed in the United States of America

5  4  3  2  1

CIP data appear at the end of the book

*Acknowledgments*

Grateful acknowledgment is made to the following journals in which some of
the poems in this book first appeared, sometimes in different versions: *The
Journal*: "Snowfall"; *The New Republic*: "Necklace," "Salver," "Slum Corner";
*The Paris Review*: "Among Appliances"; *Partisan Review*: "Three Cradle
Songs"; *Poetry*: "A Luddite Lullaby," "Romanesque," "Tableau"; *Salmagundi*:
"The Nudes"; *Shenandoah*: "The Known World"; *Stand*: "This Far"; *Western
Humanities Review*: "The Palace at Granada," "A Waiting Room in Vienna";
*The Yale Review*: "A Muse."

  My thanks to the Ohio Arts Council, the University of Cincinnati Charles
Phelps Taft Foundation, the Camargo Foundation, the Ingram Merrill
Foundation, and the National Endowment for the Arts for grants which
allowed me to complete this book.

*The publisher gratefully acknowledges the support of Lannan Foundation
in the publication of this book.*

*For Cathryn, Ted, and Anna*

# CONTENTS

I

# SLUM CORNER

On Vine Street the Dickensian splendor
of the Omega Plasma Center.
Here are your eccentrics, your waifs
in dangling mufflers and too-short topcoats,
your grizzles and stogies, distracted
mutterings, harlequin tatters in every polyester shade.
A gaggle of caricatures, they hop, mince
and shuffle in gritty December—of course
it is Christmas—from free store food
bank soup kitchen orange brick
mission of St. Francis Seraph back
here where You Can Earn $100 A Month
By Helping Others. This is the economy
of good will, Sirs. Red sap bulges
the poly bags like filled stockings.
Here are gift givers, primal humane
machines, bees drained twice a week
of their dense honey, fed on sugar water.

Would you buy used blood from this man?
Not likely. Nevertheless, he reminds you,
as the year draws to a close and thoughts turn charitable,
of the past you must always have with you.
You may hear the rattle in the cough
still distinctive, and if you manage to overlook
the slung black plastic trash bags everywhere,
the Problem of the Female Vagrant
can seem to reappear. Doddering
throwbacks, atavistic remnants multiplying
in dim passageways like roaches,
caught in the scattered commerce

of the streets—these are nothing new.
The winter sun is setting on an empire
while a cripple sweeps debris into the alley.
Roads climb hills to the same ever-retreating suburbs.
Turn on your radio. What time is it?
Are there no prisons, no workhouses?

# A WAITING ROOM IN VIENNA

Everything papered over, showing its age.
Take this bronze cage of an elevator:

directions etched on a plate in Gothic script
still decorous, a curt acknowledgment

that the porter, alas, has run off. Spindly lock,
clink of a schilling, then the ponderous rise

through layers of decaying bourgeoisie
thick as the marble floors. See how this works?

Herr Engineer, it's true, must take in boarders,
the heiress drapes her fainting couch with chintz—

but each still owns a well appointed suite.
Their paths are clear. They know they will descend

from privilege to the merely picturesque
with grace intact, abundantly propped up

by high dark corridors imbued with wax,
ubiquitous clocks and beds as big as sloops.

Who could imagine it any other way?
A spread of *things*, stolid, hierarchical,

surrounds them like a mulch. Yes, things catch dust,
but even that keeps up appearances

and garnishes their style. Within the nest
of flats, streets, squares, boutiques, and ateliers

enfolding the private core, the past is free
to rot and grow. Cafés proliferate

on ring roads built too broad for barricades,
the pillars of the domed cathedral twine

with plaster vines. In the Jugendstil decor
of the newest U-Bahn terminals, in song—

relentless waltz or vaguely genteel march,
always light-hearted, always a little sad—

time blurs its edge, is made hospitable,
and settles its bones into an overstuffed chair.

# THE PALACE AT GRANADA

*All nations have their appointed time, and when their appointed time comes they cannot keep it back an hour, nor can they bring it on.* — THE KORAN

The way they worshipped
water, its viscous
layering, what it does
to tiles, terra cotta
and cut stone, how
inside the great empty
ribcage of the hall
its bubbling refines
silence.
     Mists
from a thin jet
cool the courtyard,
a calm pool centers
its terrace. These endless
guises of the stream
amaze. Sprayed,
gurgling, or still, it holds
a protean integrity
against the crumbling
world.
     Paradise
is a walled garden.
Scents — delirious
myrtle, orange blossom
on a faint interior
breeze — inveigle the flow
of seasons. What could
define them? Cisterns

in towers, hidden
ductwork replenishing
honeycombed galleries—
all this ingenuity
to beguile.
           An empire
of surfaces. If
they felt loss,
they diffused it in
labyrinths of chambers:
a public hall, pillowed
family apartments,
the innermost vaulted salons
for women—and
the baths, where
the life was, filled
with steam and discussion,
or solitary, regal, baths
for children, for ladies
of varying station, one even
set aside for singing
girls.
    The past
is a damp touch or
an echo. It blooms
in a geometric
ceiling, enlivens
a door frame, or hints
merely in one sinuous
border, dips and goes
underground.
           History
as reverie. Voices
(you must imagine them)

rippling from far rooms,
the sultan paying tribute
to the infidel. His church
will squat in the temple,
his chattered speech
swallow their tongue.
                        What
remains is gesture:
pale columns, archways
mirroring each other,
an elegance
of attenuated yearning.
In the prayers
adorning the walls
script rises in swirls.

# ROMANESQUE

Skittering over rubble
the holy scavenger
builds from a clutch of shards.
His skull is a cracked
tureen. Untempered,
voluble, his gaze plows
the calcified distances.
His earthy cathedrals
spiral up like tendrils
sprouting from a potter's
field. He works in furrows
like his brother serf
and has no name.

History is scarified.
What he is able
to justify he will use.
He believes the acanthus
will bless his bald column,
the ram's horn reclaim.
The shattered past may yet
be fruitful. In the cells
of hothouse monasteries
its filaments devolve
to marginalia.
If he seeks illumination
he will find it in gold leaf.

God's wrath adorns the world.
His toil is deliberate
as penance. Icons loom

in the elaboration
of sanctified promises.
Groined vaults multiply,
their fractured bows extending
from dust to dust.
He is a true barbarian.
In the stone rainbow
of the arch, he has chiseled
minute replications
of his endless saints.

# SALVER

This bone china salver rimmed in gold.
A lump of earth—washed, patted,
purified, yes, but with the feel of the hand still in it,
bone burnt to white ash stirred in for strength,
trimmed and pressed to the mold.
The tall racks entering the ovens,
the poles and flat shovels
are tools to keep our own limbs out of the fire.
The long blast purges it.
Glazes clarify and seal, drawing it to a purpose.
It is set apart.

Preserved, it will preserve.
A tray for letters, a jelly dish,
a saucer for the prince's wine after a cautious foretaste—
its uses have gathered over time.
A disk of vitrified clay with a talisman in its name,
it arranges and protects.
Nothing soft need touch our fingers.
In the final stages of the finishing room
it is handled again, but lightly,
a wreath of pure value applied with a camel's-hair brush.

Completed, it will outlast us.
Flames only temper it more.
Though it crack and sink through layers of dust,
it will never blend back into earth.
Shards will announce our unfathomable civilization
long after its function is lost.

# NECKLACE

An unassuming
compound, clamped
to its purpose:
to circle
the neck.
Yet *neck* is
a peg for hanging,
*lace* a snare
or noose.
These origins
lift the caught
traitor, the cutpurse
toward us a moment,
though they are mostly
lost. The term
narrows, grows encrusted
with time. Custom
strings baubles
on the blank roots.
Here are pearls,
the product
of a more refined
context. Action
turns to ornament,
the rub
of meaning glossed
through use. This
does not stop.
Even now
in the raw usage
of the townships

the neck is
laced:
the tire, ardent
with new purpose,
hangs on the peg.

# TABLEAU

Some pure revolutionary moment—some Zapata, say,
bludgeoning open the heavy doors of the hacienda at last
and the rag-tag rabble behind him bursting in
all shouts and bandoleras among the vases on their shelves,
the still-open rosewood jewel case, the shallow drawers of the
    escritoire
where the papers had been snatched up, cool air now just
settled after the landlord's abrupt departure.
I have imagined two distinct worlds here:
outside, fields of corn, beans, cotton, and little familiar huts
in the far distance, the sun telling its old story to the dirt;
inside, sheer potential: a clawfoot tub
to be filled with pigs' blood, or a small Manet
of some Europeans in top hats ripe for slashing,
or the wine cellar, a standing invitation.

Endless possibilities—and they've all occurred—
for actions god-like and bestial, the premise of clean beginnings
held out like a snapshot. The table is set.
There are the casements that could be thrown open,
the larder full of gleanings. There are the agents
before history: not yet a vanguard, or louts, hooligan
bandidos, founding fathers, terrorists, progenitors
of a dynasty of dim, paid-off bureaucrats. In this moment
we can see men as anything they might become.
They are stopped here, at the first stage of entrance,
their boots just two footsteps away from the Persian carpets,
their hands undecided, still purposeless, jutting
stiffly from the wrists as they gawk now suddenly
transfixed before a wall of full-length mirrors.

# A MUSE

Everything that's new is old. Everything old
sags with the layered distortions of our looking.
Sad, baggy world, the past in its nostalgic hats
no one ever wore, stacks of gloves and roiling hemlines,
stumbles with the burdens we've heaped up over
its plundered core.
                        Look at her—
she can't tell day from night and, wandering,
she turns up everywhere. She feels at home,
is always wrong. When dawnlight finds her
propped in a doorway, she seems anomalous
yet comfortable, a bizarre lost cousin
whose name we can't recall.
                              What if
she sleeps on grates, bathes in the library?
She is bold, oblivious, a spirit
of indiscriminate accumulation. Heroes, gods,
wars and glories, whatever we forget
is in her weaving. Shiftless, ever resourceful,
she blesses us.
                    So the high-tech space fantasy
glowing on the screen gets sprinkled
with villainous Gothic dwarfs, Restoration
masks on sticks for decadence, and robots
with scimitars. So the slave-owning neoclassical founders
are conjured to fine-tune the Republic.
Anything goes. In the free dream of anachronism
she skirts the edge of the trash compactor,
gorged with its droppings, finding her tattered filigree
in the dappled remains.
                          Don't stare—

she wears your speculation like a nightgown.
The eyelet trim is dangling, the silk belt
droops a frayed tail. When wind cuts
through the peignoir's multiplying peek-a-boos
she winks, alert in her cast-offs,
promising once again the comfort
of something you've never seen.

# THE NUDES

*Who are these coming to the sacrifice?*


Consider them templates or blank keys,
pure, a little distant, yet always blatant
in the numberless duplications to which they are subject.

When we see them as Greeks—and it is
perhaps too easy to do this—they are adepts at the temple.
Their limbs columns, shoulders the perfect bases

of pediments. They are all male and on their way
to slaughter a garlanded cow.
This ideal cut in damp clay, in marble—

even the pubic hair bunched in symmetrical leaves
to border the isolate stalk.
We can follow that procession, we have

marched in it. But here, if there is a goal at all,
it is to linger, endlessly, in a chamber
if we choose to see them this way—and again,

it is not hard, letting the mind meander
to Orientalia. Odalisque. The concept
of abundance, composed in lustrous oils:

skin rounding in a kind of relief almost, to the breasts
and languorous belly, genitals secret
under waves of thigh. Bodies

with no angles—only ripples, pulsing,

we might imagine, from some inexhaustible core.
No purpose but dalliance.

Silent forms, on vases or stretched cloth—
see how their stasis feeds our hunger?
They are mirrors showing nothing but our own desire.

If we look again, thinking—though this is harder—
of limbs floating into paper beneath the chemical bath,
and if we see now both sexes emerge and

the lines and the chamber, are we closer?
Heads, shaved or sprouting fuzz,
cheek hollows, ribs, other clefts and protrusions

rendered to a gloss of filings,
black on white. The process of abstraction
relentless in print after print.

It anchors our vision. Staring
for hours into the resolving pools,
we slowly begin to approach

the necks and awkward shoulder blades,
the hands dropped in a vestige of shame
we can hardly comprehend.

# SNOWFALL

The long park. February. A snow gale.
The boy in the red parka walking there.
Halfway between the rink and the ballfield
he stops. The fast snow makes him a pink blur.
Bootholes behind him, filling, the hard chill
that holds him, and this pure world rimmed in fur.

He is inside it now. All he can feel
is set against the sameness everywhere:
cloudy drifts to his knees, snow dropping still
from the still blank sky impossibly near
and far, horizonless, deepening, sealed.

What are the limits of memory? A figure
trudging through nothing stops. The white field fills
with detail: eyebrows frosted, muffled ears
buffeted by gusts, damp breath through wool
as distances draw close. On boundless air
impressions are drifting in great twining reels
like new stars, flaring, ephemeral
within the thickening fall.

# A RIDE

Sweet corn just papyrus shocks now along the roadside,
knotted clumps of tomato vines,
the river a rippled brown margin glinting back
low angles of sun that make everything look clear.
Summer was too long. We live too far south.
But winding over the small hills on the Kentucky side of the
    water
I can take in this late October ease like breaths of ripe air
tinged with the dust smell of leaf piles and apples stacked at the
    fruit stand.

Tell me, Nostalgia, how many memories are we making today
as Anna and Teddy scramble down the pumpkin hill again,
each orange globe a shout against the fading grass?
A wasp plunders a bruised winesap by the turban squash.
Videotape hums in the camcorders as minivans load and depart,
full of gourds and domesticity, for the blond suburbs.
Lugging our sacks, I am fatherly, autumnal.

I remember the soft pleasure in these cycles that never seem to
    change,
how it rests on the kids playing Twenty Questions in the
    backseat,
in the light catching a swirl of my wife's hair above her
    cheekbone.
Through the windshield the peeling township post office and
    the shacks staggering toward the river
are a genre painting. On the far hills fat sheaves of burley
cure in the black half-open tobacco barns.

When we reach the ferry, the river's yellowed with the sunset.

The auburn shag and watery eyes of the ferryman
gleam like the final product of a dozen generations.
Sixteen, happy to be employed, he spins the big iron wheel,
leaps like a dancer from the tug to the barge and back.

# THIS FAR

Our house a child's picture of a house:
brick box with a thick half-timbered hat,
fat porch supports, a fussy privet skirt
girding the chipped limestone foundations.
Squat, bürgerlich, the bay-windowed dining room
is bigger than any other in the house.
And why not? The entry with its blunt statement
of stair, a modern ashless gas fireplace,
and pocket doors protecting a tidy parlor
are fairly obvious. Halls that bud
square rooms say, *Sleep here. Put the crib here.*
*Work here in this room set aside for work.*

When they built this house the middle class was rising
from cholera. Their workdays simmered in the basin,
but at dusk they'd cross the canal and catch a breeze
of incline railroad to waft them home uphill.
The first commuters. Proprietors of small shops
and oversized families, men ponderous as Taft
whom they admired. Their sons half-dandified,
daughters wanting the vote — at least the house
was sensible. Shouldered next to neighbors,
it huddled where it belonged: in the shadow
of the dying beer baron's protuberant estate,
all cupolas and steamboat balconies.

Imagine his marvelous airy parties
summers when our block was an echo in his woods.
There were servants becoming quietly unaffordable
and an oompah band from the Turnverein below.
If it was clear, you could look out over the brick clutter

past hills tangled with grapes and the mud-slowed river
to horse pastures beyond—whole layers of vision.
And the house itself hand-carved: lintels, hearths,
even the doorknobs gorged. This opulence
thins as it replicates. Our stained pine floors,
the arbor sagging in the small backyard,
aimed for a reasonable elegance.

That grace, like the rose pane over our window,
has faded to mere comfort. The baron's home
is split into flats, but his name still rides our street.
It peeks from the froufrou of nostalgic labels
in stacks of six-packs. It will live forever.
The houses will stand for another ninety years
aging to distinctiveness, their plans
more plain as they are altered. When I sit
sipping on the porch, looking out at the street
and the other porches like cages open to the day,
I can understand the child-like satisfaction
in climbing just this far.

# AMONG APPLIANCES

They are so busy and self-involved as I hear them muttering in
    the distance
that they strike me sometimes as sheer marvels:
the dishwasher filling its huge blue gullet—a cluck from the
    timer,
and spindly wings spew out scalding water in the dark—
or its basement cousin chugging yet another load through the
    changes,
whirling, rocking, belching gray suds and lint into the concrete
    washtubs.

Though I can never keep track of them all, I'm charmed by the
    cycles:
their varied lengths, sudden shifts and rigorous sense of time,
the control knob simple as a windup clock, language of click
    and whir,
mysterious pauses while something is draining or filling,
or silence even while something is gathering strength.
There's a music in these risings and fallings—odd rest,
    crescendo, diminuendo—
the soothing predictable pattern of potential and release.

I am no technophile, not all machines give this comfort.
Our vacuum cleaner is a ball and chain that growls as you try to
    make it work,
I have never wanted a yard big enough to need a power mower,
and lamps I have always thought of as most useful when
    unnoticed
like a perfectly attendant butler wearing a small hat.

I like the ones that have their own intricate lives—

not too private or powerful, like the bank machine that calls you
    by name and suddenly gulps your card,
nothing fussy or intimidating, nothing imitating a person,
but the stolid non-interactive types that work for years,
    supporting the whole household:
the refrigerator shuddering to keep cold then deciding—who
    knows when?—to defrost itself,
the furnace drumming up flames, beating a hot breeze through
    the frilly cast iron vents,
the dryer tumbling socks and lingerie in a blurred luxurious
    jumble.
All these big boxes with their timers and thermostats,
defining the stages of their tasks, devouring what I feed them,
pulling the current up through the basement meter.

It is shameful but sometimes I want them all on.
I set the controls and leave, like an absent deist god,
but am also content to work among them with a broom or
    sponge for a time,
a robot master tidying up around laborious metal lives.

# PALM

It seems, in this light,
to leap for joy:
its inner stalks, twice as tall as a man,
shooting up from the center like fireworks,
bowing finally to gravity only at the very top;
the outer ones, reaching from a deeper point
in broader curves sagging with the light, starting
to explode in yellow khaki,
as if the trunk were a powder keg, a pineapple
grown enormous, timed to go off before my eyes.

Stalk after stalk
in repeated extravagant gestures
with all the flamboyance of a transplant eager to please.
Each parallel blade takes the same tack:
needled to the stem, then broadening to a saber and thinning
    again
to a knife point, a stickpin, a split hair.
Fresh green at the base thrusts
toward olive as it opens, tightening to a wisp of burnt redwood
at the tip. As the sun lifts,
the whole arrangement slices itself in shadows.

Such intricacy—blade, stalk, and half-hidden bloom
each catching a different side of the light.
At heart, though, it is blunt as a dinosaur.
The rawhide barrel plopped square on the dirt just a storage tank
studded with sockets of dropped-off limbs,
the center a thicket of stilettos,
and all the lofty foliage fierce and inedible.
Simple, unyielding, it sucks breath from the air,

tugs up the odd rain and jumps
again and again at the sun.

The same stalk lifting and falling, aging over and over
through the same course of colors—
the palm keeps re-telling what it was and is.
Abundance is a fountain where every changing stage
fans out at once as I watch.
In this light, circled by a gravel path,
the outer bulk makes a sundial.
Inside, a bouquet of grassy blossom
nestles among dry sockets and new spikes
as if in the crook of an arm.

# NEW FATHER

Loose in the dark, she made a shifting lump
under covers, playing between us in the bed:
invisible fish, rising to my touch
like flesh — then a sudden frog-kick,
somersaults prodding the taut outer sack.
Nights grew thick with her. By early spring
you loomed above me in the bedroom light,
a great boat of fertility and desire,
sweat-prowed, cresting the waves. We jostled her.

She wriggled back, tickling our dreams. In yours
she came in the shape of a boy, grinned up at you,
and didn't hurt. In mine she would arrive
in a half-abandoned airport, able to speak.
Vague destinations sputtered on the P.A.
as they wheeled you out to the departure gate
under a row of skylights. I remember
nurses checking our tickets, then her birth
as effortless as opening a door.

Hello. Her fingers spread. I heard the words
she planted in my mind that lumpy night,
as if to prepare us for other nights to come:
*Look! Look at the light!* Then I woke —
or slipped, it seems now, into a watery time
of half-naps, stunned dawns, rising to her clock
and yours, and swimming back to find each other
in pools of late-summer dark, our whole stretched world
orbiting the damp moons of your breasts.

# INVOCATION

Powers I can understand
only in the touch of dark,
the torchlight of familiar skin
flaring till the last return
to rest—fill this house.

Walls that hold us room to room,
nest of bed and crib, each face
hiding the day's loss, each mask
of sleep—these fragile surfaces
suffuse and heal.

In the cracked light of the day
voices scour, flesh turns dry
as chalk, my turned back seals its cage
of bone on abstract rage refined,
glinting alone.

Tunneled halls, room on room,
facets caught inside a gem,
lead me off. I feel each step
split a new edge from the stunned
interior.

Only darkness dims that prize
at last, and shows me what I'd lost.
Habits loosen to desire,
all the dear worn gestures grow
supple, renewed.

Keep the dark close. Let me keep

treasuring what I forget
too soon: our warming hands, the house
they build again each night that holds
us in its arms.

# THREE CRADLE SONGS

Norman Dinerstein, composer
1937–1982

When sowers scatter wind
under the whirling sun
burlap sacks catch
the light's motion.
The rocking glide of work
and slowing clock of flesh
round the day. When seed
tumbles like a wish
on darkening air it sings
what no one hears.
At work's end the field
is stars.

\*

In a waking house: the first alert
rap of coffee on the tongue, fit
of the mug's familiar handle, winter light
fresh through kitchen windows, the half-burnt
smell of toast filling the room—morning
in its various common songs: linoleum
creaking underfoot, the saucepan's thrum,
the small precise egg timer ringing and ringing

\*

This dim aubade. A chorus of chummy frogs would be better.
Or wild bells. Or a kind of skitter faster than a rag.
Dry notes for the tongue's brandy, the warm skull's glittering
eyes.
Memory's a thin score. Time dulls the timbre.
Our labor: to pluck, scrape, pound, wrestle a fluid voice—
the beautiful imperfect work that will not bring you back.

# A LUDDITE LULLABY

*On every hand, the living artisan is driven from his workshop, to make room for a speedier, inanimate one.* — CARLYLE


The curve of the hand fits the tool,
has grown to it. The path of the scythe
swings the arms. As a spindle turns,
your fingers dance, dear,
in flickering tallow light.
The infant sleeps and all for your delight.

      His breath is a slow stream pressing forward.
      His growth, if he should survive, rides on its current
      in the changing flood.

The push of the river lifts the millwheel,
is spent in drops. The ploughman's dray
shies at the whistle now, as you rise
in dark and the infant stirs, dear,
but does not wake. The street
is filled with dawn, and all for your delight.

Why do they rise in my dreams, the hands
walking off sleep as they follow the rows
of houses down to the mill? Do I think
I can make the stream flow back, dear,
give Jack his old work, and set
you back by the cradle, all for your delight?

      In the changing flood they ride on a current.
      Swirled to a slow eddy pressing forward,
      weavers lift and sink in a breath.

The whir of the millwheel drowns the day's wreckage,
speeds the turning spool. Smashed looms
cradle the pickerel. When dark comes
the mill will let you go. Sleep, dear,
as an infant sleeps through the night,
rocked on the water, all for your delight.

III

# THE KNOWN WORLD

*Every epoch not only dreams the next one, but also, in dreaming, strives towards
its awakening. It carries its own end within itself and unfolds it with artifice ...*
— WALTER BENJAMIN, "Paris, Capital of the Nineteenth Century"

*Et leur chanson se mêle au clair de lune*


Progress as the history of wheels:
endless tethered circles round the gin pit,
the measured creak of leather, harness clank,
clops, and pulley whining the day's lumps up:
heat in a horsecart, its wood rims nicking
on cobblestone. Or millstone grinding
the corn you rolled to the mill, the millwheel churned
in the swirls of the millrace. Paddlewheel
cutting steps in froth. Phaeton, brougham,
the singular conveyances of squires —
his light whip, your lordship, barely a question mark
before the iron arm jerks on its axis,
wrenching a grooved wheel over cinders,
spikes, the ties that bind lines for the wheels
of commerce: black funicular tugging hands
from the pit, the wheel to her very own treadle,
my dear, in the long hall, wheels of ships, and hidden wheels
that shut the vault's door or lift a glittering
chandelier over the wheel of heads that turn
the hopes of the world: Empire, a massy wheel
fixed on the summit of the highest mount,
outposts, colonies, explorations that thrust
a brave torch into the cave — and its walls are lined
with diamonds — the wheel hefting our white
burden, its dark spokes pulsing with goods, fleets
belting horizons, within its rim

round faces, food, fuel, nations, all debts
forgiven, your one mad whirling dynamo and
frivolous velocipede.

*

*The wagon lit was glazed with ice. The master's voice*
*pinned us on air—such sweet French*
*with the odd gruff echo of St. Petersburg.*
There is no gravity *(this hooded,*
*a growl).* Invisible strings there are,
lifting your body, so. We *almost flew.*

*

Damp woods edge the sanatorium.
Lovers must come here, to pick
mushrooms now. Spruce and hemlock dripping
from a cool drizzle, the crawling shadows
under wet stones, gray heads half bent,
quizzical. To think of the delicate fingers
plucking them from soil,
each fat tube of stem lifted
with a hollow tug, its tip a spread
umbrella, a cowl. Parts flop
in their baskets: gills, fleshy
excrescences, flumes, filaments—
all the miniature channels, fronds, and sacs—
a dusting of spores. Now
he is lifting her to her mount

and she adjusts herself, I know,
and the hooves are beginning
to clatter far beyond this window.
It is raining now, drenching
them, her blood
is up, her fevered
breath thin quick
puffs, the mushrooms tangled in the saddlebags
bounce on the flanks.


\*


lead to the inescapable conclusion that what we may best
describe as "the strategic faint" served at least two
distinct purposes: while demonstrating beyond doubt that
the lady in question possessed those attributes pertaining to
a uniquely feminine sensitivity, it likewise permitted a
sudden and complete retreat from awkward or unsavory
circumstances—a breathing space, as it were.
Thus the collapse of Lady Attley upon the untimely
arrival of Sir Malcolm at their box, assorted whispers and
consequent swoons during the intricate pas de deux that
followed, and the predictably histrionic tottering and fall
of milady's maid on the unexpected appearance of her mistress
    under
cover of night may be considered to illustrate a chain reaction of
    spontaneous
yet not entirely unrehearsed responses to particular difficulties.
It should, indeed, be noted that a significant
number of such attacks of light-headedness were no doubt
    induced or at
the very least augmented by those rigid implements of

fashion preferred by the sex for the modest concealment and
definition of their delicate forms, such dual purpose reflecting
most clearly a pattern of control and abandon parallel to
that of the faint itself—we speak, of course, of "stays."
In most cases the loosening of these whalebone devices,
    allowing
as it did for the restoration of respiratory activity adequate
to the scene at hand and granting a momentary respite for
deliberation, was sufficient to ensure the victim a regained
composure and, as an often unforeseen consequence, provide
for many men the first surprising glimpse of the "unbridled"
    female torso since
infancy, with results that may well become the object of further


*



Land.
Interest and rents.
On 'Change.
Lady B., Founder of the Charitable Societies
Mills: as of iron, cotton, grain
Mines.
Monsignor in his summer vestments
Import-Export
Mistress of the house, bright spirit, his better self
Railroads.
The Retired Major General
Matthew Reynolds, M.A., Fellow of the Institute
Our own decorous invalid, her wicker chair wheeled near the
    sea
Secretary to the Minister
The Maritime Assurance Society of the Port of Marseilles

barristers, magistrates, other wigs and benches
a first-rate inspector of granaries
Counting Houses.
P. LaPointe, Purveyor of Optical Instruments
Distinguished fellow members of the Inquisitors Club, honored
    guests
Dr. Forceps
Mrs. Gridley's Establishment for Young Ladies
Munitions.
yeomen, sheriffs, singing blacksmiths
an agent of the redoubtable Sir Joshua
Inspector Houndstooth
chief clerk hunched on the high stool
her dressmaker, madam
accomplished and talented, adept at the pianoforte, conversant
    in the modern languages, of most refined character and ready
    at once to assume the management of a small household
Reginald Threadbare, tutor to the next Lord Hawley
dubious would-be naturalists
Discoverers of the Pole
artists, dancers, etc.
Artistes.
Your Genial Host
V. Cacon Surgical Appliances
Service: steward butler valet cook lady's maid maid-in-waiting
    parlormaid chambermaid kitchenmaid driver groom
    gameskeeper stable boy scullion
tradesmen
vendors of fruit
Ruined.
ruined ruined ruined


*

Take China. Open the door
and in goes the opium. Like
a jewel box, like an ampule, like a pillow
full of feathers. All nations
nosing the waking harbor:
cacophony of stacks, flagged
messages, winches creaking great wrapped
bundles into the gaping holds.
Will, diplomacy, appetite:
the early bird thus fur-lines
his nest. You may sign the bill
of lading over Peking duck. Coolies
half-dozing on layered pallets—let
sleeping dogs lie.

Or the "dark" continent. If you
shoulder your burden—or, better still,
leave that to the bearers—
you pull out a sack of diamonds.
Or gold. Or ivory. Or anything that
gleams. One hundred coils
of copper wire, seventy bolts
Manchester cotton in eight standard colors,
fifteen hundred fundos of bubu beads equal
mineral rights. Thus free trade. Thus
development, the conversion of benighted souls
to the one True Path. Arduous, yes,
but have no doubt: they will, one day,
see the light.

*

*Alphonse, I have discovered,*

*is a fool. His tireless jetés tire me.*
*All that thrust and manly bravado,*
*predictable as an engine. In the end*
*he becomes a mere standard,*
*a shaft on the carousel. I spin*
*alone around my own center.*
*The master, it is said, finds him*
serviceable—he leaps but will never soar.


\*


Observe the latest Pole
ascending to the stage.
Exquisite, fashionable,

he keeps the common touch—
and melts every genteel
heart. How he can reach

into our very souls!
That torrent of moustache
across a broad profile,

those peasant eyes, a blush
of passion tingeing pale
high-boned cheeks—such

beauty, fierce yet noble,
enchants a jaded age.
As he stands before the hall

our brows grow feverish

with longing. We can feel
in the first faint brush

of his fingertips a whole
world: One Holy Church,
one homeland! Languid trills

lure us to the edge
of tears. His hands recall
plains, streams, a heritage

of innocence that still
must live there, to emerge —
only in loss. Ah, febrile

yearning for the rich
unattainable!
He speaks our language.


*


New lines belching suburbs. Where
a cheese seller edges the slag heap
rickety cottages sing the rails.
A neoclassical bank branch
imitates a temple. The mews totters,
its aging mares dreaming in soot.
Coughing behind thin doors,
endless hawking of goods in lanes,
sweeps calling—*Step here, Sir!*—clank and
sizzle of the forge—all swallowed now
in the long whistle that scatters

shacks, shops, homes, carts, and offices:
a petulant child's suddenly discarded toys.

\*

We see you. This is a new
system. You are separate.
Boxed, hence untainted. Except
for the sins that have stained you
already. These time burns out.
You turn the wheel—many wheels
connected, turned by fellows
like you you cannot see. But
we see them. We oversee.
As here in chapel the Lord
oversees each private flawed
soul. In its pew. You are free.
Barred from transgression. His day
awaits us all. Let us pray.

\*

*Wearied, I consider the Lilies of the field—*
*and of the salons and the boudoirs and*
*a thousand other places. They blossom*
*each night in the boxes, positively*
*determine the season.*
*Even the Empress affects their flirtatious grace.*

*Those layers of silk, lace, crinoline—*

*how can they move?*
*While I stretch and point, they*
*spin in the world's eye:*
*grand balls, the Bois, the smart*
*maisonnette in the last hours before dawn —*
*an endless whirl, all with the same breathless*
*poise. Their art is a fleeting*
*balance. Their toil, like mine,*
*the appearance of ease.*

*

Secede sign my manifesto denigrate
small minds shopkeepers warders of cultural
culture fig leaf bestowers cultivate masters

Cultivate a medieval grace carve that
frame flatten the scene to design to
points paint light paint strokes paint paint

Paint in Montmartre no on this harsh
coast here in the parks no back
stage in the open air in my studio

Study martyrdom act like a beast like
a bourgeois play the dandy the pederastic
aristocrat recluse raving monk

Rave in a garret starve on the street
corner in a stuporous café sipping
plonk brandies absinthe filling the glass

Your full bodied mistress forgives her pillow
forgets it sags it fills with scorn for
scorn forgotten in the fullness of time

＊

Why is Pierrot sad?
Because his sleeves have outgrown him.
Why is the moon sweet?
Because the soft lute sings.
Who sails for Cythera?
Time has dimmed the names.
What of this parchment fan?
It tells no story.
This yellowed bow and flounce?
Take us away.
Why is Harlequin rude?
Who plucks these fading strings?
Why does the boat glide?
Moonlight soothes the water.
What is the dim stirring?
Mist's echo.
That distant tripping dance?
Follow.
Is this the shore?
The old moon sleeps in a shell.
Where are the masks?
Sea-tossed.
Where is the sweet pavilion?
Whose dreams are these?
Why does the dark lute sing?

Waiting

Stumbling through
night fog, fingering
pages, curled photos—fruit
man, drayman, are
you, carver in the
carvery of a fine hotel, the idle
Prince of Wales, waiting

Bearded faces all
masks, reflections in
display windows, red
lanterns of is it an
abattoir, waiting

Feeling my
way down the old
lanes veins runnels of the
flesh, what
place is, waiting

Sinking through dark
textures, wool
smother, muslin, webby
lacework sudden
upthrust of bone where
are you I
stop some where waiting
                              I'm Jack.
Your one-man staggering facts-and-figures library

of goings-on by night. Your Domesday Jack. Tarts? I know how
    many,
where, when, who, how old, how much for what, how sick, who
got what from whom when. And I know you.
The cut of your beard, your pipe, where you wait, each detail
    insinuates
an entire world of taste. This one wants a wild beast, that a great
lady fallen on hard times, a dancer, pert gamin, naughty child.
Naughty, naughty! Please dear, you must spank this nasty wild
banker for diddling your clean petticoats. And, of course, she
    will.
Buyers can be choosers in this market. Whitechapel
is one long night-counter—be careful what you pick!
You must be curt, fastidious. I know what I don't like
and dump it in the alley. All gone. Gentlemen, your rustlings
of silk, scented would-be mysteries, your bustles
like waddling pillows, peekaboo camisoles, layered stays
barbaric as gargoyles leering with hooks and eyes—
all these sweet dandlings, Sirs, rest at last in the ragman's sack.
When you creep home to your upright motherly wives,
    remember Jack.

    *

*To be aware, at all times, where you are, yet*
*give yourself to music—to mere air,*
*finally: puffed, beat, scraped*
*into vibration. My shoes meet the floorboards*
*with a thrust the whole body*
*has memorized.*
        *And forgotten—no, a secret*
*I know but can't tell, there*

*in the muscles, working*
*like blood. Technique: sharp,*
*clear, smooth, a gem of ice that*
*frees me. Friction is a lie.*


\*


A certain familiarity with the materials.
And simple tools. And
the leisure awarded after a day spent copying orders
for trusses or selling woolens or presiding at the high window
of a ticket booth. And the instructions for assembly in their
decorous but functional prose. The ability
to read such instructions. The wages not
dissolved immediately in gin or thinned by deductions for tools
    rent
debts at the company store or kept aside
for the invalid grandmother or hidden in a locket hung
around the neck for burial fees.


To instill some measure of pride in individual
craftsmanship. And provide diversion
for lives bounded increasingly by work which is repetitious
and spiritually numbing. To create beauty
in the modest home. And
socialism. To construct one decorous but
functional oak-and-cushion chair easily
adjustable to any taste and suitable for instructive
leisure reading in the small parlor under
the lamp's cozy glow near the mauve-flowered umbrageous
Arthurian wallpaper.

*

This fierce archaeology
disturbs. A hunger for new
old settings, still more chambers

to the tomb, musty plunder —
you can't tell what you're after.
All that debris: curls,

long strips and shavings planed off
by the scraper — are these stages
in a liberation? The papers' beige

geometries thin to cottages, dim
sunbursts and at last thick-petalled
jungle blossoms big as sunflowers.

Unrestrained, obscure,
these night-blooming tuberoses still
entice. They are stripped

inexplicable secrets: violet
engorgements, damp folds of umber
and ultramarine, a thicket

of leafy conjecture.
When you slice through the wall's flat
hedgerow, it leaves a scar.

Whitewash it. For exteriors
scalding water, lye soap, bleach or
astringent acids, as a last resort

sandblasting which pocks the surface
and is thus not always suitable.
Nothing is suitable.

Time stains, disguises:
pale lintels steeped through coal years
to the color of peat, red brick

gone sooty or repeatedly painted red.
You scrub, chip, and peel. Grit
powders, sifts through air, drifts and

catches, troubling a wheezing lung.
An endless scratching at cornice
and pediment, frantic

as a prisoner's. Dusty treasures,
hieroglyphs indistinguishable
from your own hand.

\*

We are in a dark place. We
see dawn only in thinning
shadows, sunset in high streaked
clouds. Time is flat. It circles

the cobbled square. Colonnades
stare at each other. Behind
the facade our galleries
wind to chambers. Consider

the walls' cool sweat, layers of
breath, nook, ledge, and bench — these our
furnishings. Habits claim them
like a moss. Sit. Listen. Forks

nicking on tin, a chair leg
wrenched across the floor — the dulled
murmur of families seeps
from the ducts. Nothing echoes

in these little rooms. Mirrors
fog with your breathing. Will you
tell us at last what we owe?
Tell us what we owe.


\*


A horse and cart is a delivery vehicle
A man with a valise is a delivery vehicle
Here are the wheels grinding the frozen plain
Here the brick factory drilling the bore
The hot shot cools in the mold
Here is your cousin speaking with captains of industry
The caricature anarchist is a delivery vehicle
Here is a smoking bowling ball with a fuse
The royal seal pressed in fresh red wax
Here we go marching through streets gates great triumphal
    arches town squares
A skittish bicycle is a delivery vehicle
The duke's full regalia fresh pressed for the review
Here are the light brigades horse marines gay fusiliers

Here is a means of full employment
The wheels of the delivery vehicle rust in pink slush
Here we are my dear with but slight inconvenience
Here is the map like a red dance
One languorous handshake is a delivery vehicle
Here is your velvet-lined box
There are the boxes pitting the frozen plain
The horse and cart the straw the thrilling escape by night
Here is entertainment of the highest order
Your cousin's yacht is a delivery vehicle
Your valise my dear your maidservant manservant presser of
    clothes
Here we go marching to the day's machines
Full employment is a delivery vehicle
A red brick factory making red bricks
The duke's cousin's royal delivery vehicle
Here they are stacked on the frozen plain
Here we are cooling in the mold
Here is a hushed note from the ambassador


   *


Secrets of the earth.
                 Burn them.
Turf nicked out, tugged off
the surface with a scream of roots:
a hunk of the bog asmolder
behind your grate.
                Older still,
coal. Asleep past the vegetal,
refining a slow
heat. Dense, mineral

ardor.

       The miner's hearthchair
was sacred. Boots
warmed by the banked ash
all night, dark lungs shuffling
toward dawn.

          Nightsoil.
Raw, corrosive, it
defiles. Quick, crush it under-
foot, bury that harsh
nitric life.

       You could
cook with it, if you
had to. Dung of the scrawny
sacred cow a marketable
basic fuel.

       The lower
orders: warm humus.
Spontaneous combustion
of a bundle of rags sleeping
in a doorway.

         That compost
is always on fire. Tiny
revolutions in the packed
organic stew, bounded,
controllable.

        Yet these are holy
mysteries: silver filings set
to a corona overnight
in your drawer — a dark
implied sun —

         unknown
light that marks the lungsacs,
weight so quick and

protean it exists only
in combination.
>                    You will
sift the pitchblende, dear lady,
reduce to purity that one
unseen glow of earth, faint
growing ripple
>                    in the blood.


\*


Mon Cher,
>                    But of course I am always delighted to hear
news—sad as it may be—from our beloved (alas, benighted!)
homeland. And to rebuke the fair bearer of such grim tidings
like the ancient tyrant?—Misha, you mistake me.
I have not been so long in this city of poets, composers,
and other fashionable aesthetes as to have thrown away
my reason or my soul.
>                    Poor Peter Ilyich! We live,
it seems, in dark times. These secret societies with their
temples, ceremonies, backward handshakes, trick rings, codes
of honor (honor, indeed, that can lead a tormented soul
to its own demise)—how I despise them!
>                    But enough. My work
is much the same: the girls adept but a bit ponderous, the boys
still affecting that dated heroic passion which looks, oddly,
mechanical. (Can you believe it, I sometimes see the entire
ensemble as a steam train: all grease and noise, hot gas, rocker
>    arms,
and simply enormous wheels—pray God we get somewhere!)
>                    Yes the parties

dazzle and, yes, I may have become perhaps the least bit
jaded. But these countesses, you know, with their revolving
paramours, the flocks of ever more praised (and ever younger!)
    breast-
thumping artists, coquettes, rich anarchists, those ubiquitous
Poles plotting nationalism or stroking the ivories or furiously
    (always
furiously) applying their energies to science—really,
it is all a bit dizzying.
                        And terribly refined, you
may be sure. If I am obliged at times to play the hirsute
primitive, God knows it comes as a relief! I long (secretly,
of course) for the barbarous mother tongue, and have even
    been—once,
I freely admit it—to the church. So you see, my boy,
I have not yet gone completely astray.


        *


In the end a fixation on ephemera.
The smoker transfixed by the way the meerschaum's curve
complements the curve of smoke, the way
the dying purple iris seem to grow
from their peacock blue vase, the way the frame
deftly entwines its flat medieval scene.
His lingering attention, thin, consumptive,
veils each object till the glowing edge
of memory begins to flare. Absinthe,
talk like wine forever on the tongue,
rain-pocked alleys, winking jets of gas,
the livid Metro's sinuous entrances
a summons to the pit. Delirium:

hashish paints a self-portrait, La Lune
and the rooms upstairs, night voyages
past street arabs, apaches, wrought iron blooms
caressing a maiden's thigh. Paralysis
blossoms. The long-lashed eye of the fly trap,
the pitcher's languid fluted lips—turn
your back on the dying age, these alone entice.

\*

*To think of the child who makes my shoes
in her workroom . . . A garret? A windowless
hall? Invisible. Not that one watching
from the wings (I love her blatant stare), not
Clara or a pixie or a darling baby swan.*

*What can I possibly know of her?*

*I picture a needle, thread, her fingers,
arms curving down to cradle
my bleeding feet. Handwork of dreams:
glass slippers, billowing gauze, a cat's pads
or a doll's gross pumps. For one night
scuffing on pink satin—imagine—
and toss the stained tools away.*

\*

a. The bachelor logician adores little girls.
b. All logical propositions are true.

c. Some of the pictures in the photograph album shock nannies.
d. Every nanny takes care of children.
e. Some little girls float in punts on the gentle river.
f. The book about the little girl shows that nannies are always
   wrong.
g. All men are mortal.
h. The girls in the gasworks have big wrists and cannot read.
i. All of the pictures in the photograph album are of little girls.
j. The bachelor logician is a man.
k. Nannies do not have children.
l. Some of the girls in the photograph album have narrow wrists,
   trim ankles, and pale thighs.
m. All true books confer immortality.
n. No one in the gasworks has a nanny.
o. The bachelor logician photographs all girls who float in his
   punt on the gentle river.
p. Nothing in the book about the little girl is true.

    1. Who takes care of the little girl?
    2. Who is immortal?
    3. Which pictures in the photograph album are true?

*

Dreams of the grand constructors, genius
engineers! Their tracks are everywhere—
bright parallels stapled on the landscape, reaching
toward infinity over deserts under rivers around still
malarial swamps through mountains of coal.
The terminal an iron cathedral for
the worship of turning wheels, the palace
of glass, castle of factory bricks.

Nothing but what is massive, graceful
in the sheer bulk of its achievement—
O beautiful railway bridge of the silvery Tay!—
and layered with confident re-inventions
from the rifled past: the dowager Empress
as Ceres on a fat plinth, the royal head
bronze-laureled, forty feet high.

Yet there is delicacy too, in unexpected
places: pastel greens on the lacework
of bound cables drooping like vines,
the geometric dance of light in high gables,
the curve of the pissotière—everything lifts
and disperses in air. Consider further
the pure autonomy of the ponderous.
That span conveying apparently substantial carriages
toward us over the water is supported, finally,
only by itself. Near it, the skeletal tower
extends to no purpose but its own proof.

&ast;

Leaning my bicycle against a wall,
I'd wander alleys, peering into the glass
of shop windows for hours it seems, half lost,
half following the instinct of a chord
still unresolved in daydreams.
                              Boulevards
repelled me with their symmetry. I sought
fleeting visions: two housemaids sharing a blush,
a tailor grinning up from his gray board,

that blur of life in courtyards just before
chipped doors hide it away.
                              I rehearsed
the melancholy charm of work undone,
worshipped the great, imagined a supreme
unending lyric grace. The city's song
of echoes, hints, rests, scarcely heard motifs
entranced my isolate soul.
                              Tracing its ways
one afternoon, I stumbled into a square
thronged with delights: tumbrels dripping sweets,
street artists, mountebanks cajoling crowds.
A bellowing began to draw a band
of the curious. It gathered in swirls
as the lone man in the center lunged at its rim
like a tethered bear. I came near.
                              I have seen
Pierrot and parti-colored Harlequin,
those bittersweet mummers from the past,
have watched a monkey tied to a blindman's wrist,
a makeshift Punch and Judy on the run—
but never this before:
                              the man adorned
in chains, boasting as he flexed and pressed
the links into his bluish tattooed flesh,
mincing before a clamoring ring of coins,
cigarettes, loaf ends, trinkets, his cry
taunting the rickety shoulders and toothless heads
surrounding him—*I suffer! I suffer! When
shall I break free?*
                              O Masters who can spin
exquisite meandering beauty from pure air,
teach me what music lies here.

*

Rose petal tutus and the toes pumping like pistons
Every man a corsair, every woman an orchid or a swan
Refined from court ritual and, yes, the martial arts — close drill
    to fluent *corps*, jackboots to toeshoes, etc.
Break, Heart, and Limbs, Writhe in Flames!
Come on feet don't fail me now.

The edge of the diamond defines the upturned breast as the
    ribboned cravat defines the neckshaft.
Beringed hand grown fat on its cushion of coal
Your pork butcher in disguise, employer of three shop assistants
    and a wife with a dazzling lorgnette
Their Box Loge Stalls Stalls Circle Dress Circle Upper Circle
    First Balcony Second Balcony The Galleries Paradise

Dithering of the superstructure, a piffle
Flower of self-reflective mass nostalgia: fairy-tale masquerade
    balls, trotting powdered footmen, dances of dancing dolls
Romantic aristocrats and strapping peasants, an audience which
    is neither dreaming of both

*

We celebrate ourselves.
Our velvet boxes each have the very best view
of other boxes. Our privacy
is conspicuous, our taste so attuned
to the careful distinctions of the latest fashion
that if we chance to look across the hall we may see

infinite reflections of our own sensibilities.
We prefer the simplicity of the diamond,
the calm assertion of black, and modest chat free
of unseemly gestures or overt displays of feeling during the
    interval.
The rising chandelier spins this our world into facets
and scatters them over a darkening sea of heads.

To be sure, we look to all great art
for the logical extension of our values:
that a young man, infused with honor, will scale the pinnacle
of ice, brave the roaring torrent and yet, of course, weep
at the sight of his love's long lost handkerchief;
or that a lady who has bartered her virtue will descend
like a gaily colored silk,
some four hours fluttering and tossing light as it drifts
from a carelessly opened window past lintel and knocker down
to the common street. We expect
flight, great conflagrations presented on stage, murders with
    verisimilar blood
and have provided the machinery to effect these.

If, during a particular aria or pas de deux,
one's thoughts may wander with one's gaze to the darkened side
of the hall, what of that? One may even, at times, feel
confined in his box before the spectacle
like an infant too long dandled by his mother
in the demanding presence of endless—oh yes, endless—
    relatives.
The old may drift to slumber at the overture, but young hearts
caught in that close dim glow will burn
with their own fantasies set aflame by events before the
    footlights.
Dearest cousin, I see my eyes reflected like wet stars

on your bosom, in the sweet glittering ring at your throat.
Do you assume what I assume?

\*

All the world, *she says,*
knows. *But what of the world? I*
*know, the master (of course) knows,*
*and the charmed circle of soirées*
*would hardly be surprised if she*
*threw herself from a bridge or under the wheels*
*of a tram. Burdened,*
*she will sink beneath the world.*

*Already she is unseen: vague and*
*heavy as the past. She has become —*
*much too suddenly — something only*
*half-noticed, dispersed yet still*
*disturbing: in the practice room that faint*
*smell of crumpled gauze, a child*
*somewhere coughing, the ragman*
*calling in the alleys.*

\*

Enter the icehouse. Vaulted, marmoreal,
a smooth lined hole in the hillside. One snug
spike of a bolt, doors chunks of oak or quarried
limestone. Tug them aside. Here's cellarage
for seasons. What packed dirt preserves

keeps time off your muttonchop, drops a splinter
of January in your sweating glass. A fine stuffed
gallery of lost days: damp halls, faint
expiration from the calm dark slabs, drip
and hidden drain. Work stored here
as in a compressed spring. You can hear mules
grunting up the bank, curses in slurred
Welsh, pick and tongs and sledge, flesh
slipped off a palm from a sliding cake.

The river's thrust is stilled. It
serves you. Sawn off blocks of sheer
possibility. The past is stacked
in these cool storeys. You can tap them,
drag off an unwieldy hunk, or let
the entire white mountain, if you so desire,
shrink to a dribble. Come into this blank room.
Put your hand on the lugged river.

*

In moonlight who can tell
shepherdess from swan?
The shadows blur to one
grand wash. A grayish hill
flattens out within
the false proscenium
of elms. And now the spell
has fallen on the stunned
party. Revels done,
the costumes start to pale,
their hushed glimpses of skin

cool, shrink, and dim.
Is this antique style
so easily undone?
The nice distinctions
of each chosen role
are fading. Peasant, queen,
and gameskeeper have no station.
Smiles turn vague, eyes dull,
their hinting half-forgotten
or lost behind a fan.
Time stills. Old masks reveal
new ones. The hollow strum
of the lute disturbs them.
They don't know what they feel,
or if this is a scene
on stage, or if that fountain
sobbing with a will
so clear among the stones
it seems almost to shine
in ecstasy distills
everything they sense.
Their lives are painted on
a landscape. Light is still,
souls invisible.


*


Wholesale transformations. As thus: your home
becomes a villa, the mill that built your home
a castle, the workers vassals disguised
as free agents selling their health disguised
as labor. What? Try again. That retreat
looks like a peasant's cottage: thatch to retreat

70

under in mild rain, big fireplace, crude pans
on the wall. Who gets to use the pans?
Note the subtly hidden servants' quarters.
Diverse obfuscation in other quarters
as well. Sorry. Now consider this church —
or is it a town hall hunched under a church
steeple? But it's not a steeple, is it?
It's an ornate medieval bell tower and it
came from Venice. Now it's here on the grounds.
Need I mention that these well appointed grounds
resemble a museum collection of town halls?
Gothic, Romanesque, all sorts. The halls
are named for industrial magnates and men of science,
some of whom, because of their work in science,
became industrial magnates and thus could pose
as squires. Students here are able to pose
as classless, free, devoted to reason.
Confusing, yes, but useful. One reason
few students are afflicted with consumption
is that their digs only look like mines. Consumption,
rather, of knowledge of the world, of history
cooked up all around them — the history,
say, of Pre-Raphaelite art confusing
the history of painting, the confusing
study of historical fads in the housing
of squires, mills, mines, mine diseases, housing
for millhands. You understand. New masks to mirror
the past seen in the present, which is a mirror
of the past, masked and hence exotic. Thus the new
science of archaeology making the old new.
Go on, dig it up. Set the whole temple
inside the museum designed to look like a temple
and study it. Study bricks, dust, the museum
of lungs, the man studying in the British Museum
the wholesale transformation of the known world.

UNIVERSITY PRESS OF NEW ENGLAND

publishes books under its own imprint and is the publisher for Brandeis University Press, Dartmouth College, Middlebury College Press, University of New Hampshire, Tufts University, Wesleyan University Press, and Salzburg Seminar.


LIBRARY OF CONGRESS CATALOGING-IN-PUBLICATION DATA

Bogen, Don.

The known world / Don Bogen

p. cm. — (Wesleyan poetry)

ISBN 0–8195–2233–3 (cl : alk. paper). — ISBN 0–8195–2237–6 (pa : alk. paper)

I. Title. II. Series

PS3552.04337K57    1997

811'.54—dc20                                        96–38589